ARE YOU A CONFIDENT PERSON?

DR. JOHN W. MANNING

authorHOUSE

AuthorHouse™
1663 Liberty Drive
Bloomington, IN 47403
www.authorhouse.com
Phone: 833-262-8899

Published by AuthorHouse 01/13/2025

ISBN: 979-8-8230-4167-6 (sc)
ISBN: 979-8-8230-4166-9 (e)

Library of Congress Control Number: 2025900506

CONTENTS

CONTENTS

INTRODUCTION

When you see a confident person, you recognize their confidence right away. You notice it in the way they walk and hold their head up high. You hear it in the way they talk. You perceive it in the way they deal with other people. And you see it in the successes they enjoy.

I believe confidence is the key to much success and fulfillment in life, and I am glad you have chosen to take the journey toward becoming confident. Whether you view yourself as someone who is fairly confident most of the time, someone who has almost no confidence at all, or someone in between, I believe the lessons in this book will give you a greater understanding of what true confidence is and how it operates and manifests in the life of a godly person.

Confidence is a quality that make most people admire and want but sometimes struggle to develop. The good news is that confidence is a quality anyone can have. It's not like height, eye color, a beautiful singing voice, or other characteristics people are born with. Confidence is like discipline or physical strength; it can be developed. If you think, I am just not a confident person, that can change. You can be confident.... starting today.

Though confidence is often associated with people who have strong personalities, you can also be quiet and reserved, studious and serious, relaxed and laid back, yet confident at the same time. Becoming confident doesn't mean you take on a different personality. It means you become the best, most courageous, most positive version of yourself.

As you grow in confidence, you will be amazed by the possibilities that open up for you and the ways you can flourish and enjoy your life.

This first step toward confident person is to change the way you think about yourself and about God. Once you realize how God thinks about you and learn to see yourself as He sees you, confidence follow. A good pray before you go further in this book would be: "Lord, help me to grow in confidence as I come to understand how You think about me. I choose today to agree with the way You see me and, based on that I become my most confident self.

Confidence has become a buzzword in secular society-what the Bible calls "the world." Usually, when people think of confidence, they think of self-confidence. The world applauds this kind of confidence and urges everyone to develop it to the greatest possible degree.

The world often considers people with low confidence deficient in a quality necessary for success and views confidence as the solution for all kinds of problems. For example, our society says that if people aren't performing well at work or in whatever they do or if their social fife is boring, they simply need to be more confident. I wish the world knew that self-confidence isn't as valuable as many people think. It may help people accomplish certain goals, but it requires them to rely on their own strength and effort. There's a lot of striving involved in developing se lf-confidence, and striving can leave people feeling exhausted and frustrated. Reaching goals through the power of self-confidence isn't always fulfilling, so people then set new goals and drain their strength to achieve them.

DEDICATION

This book is dedicated to everyone that's having trouble with being confident within themselves and God, in ever day life, and doesn't know who they really are. I'm also dedicating this book to a very special person that's in my life, her name is: Patricia A Guillory. She encourage me every day to just have confidence in God and myself and things will be alright. She has always been an inspiration in my life. Without her being a part of my life I wouldn't have the confident I have in myself to do whatever l need to do in life. I am very grateful that I have her as a sister and a part of my life.

CHAPTER ONE

ARE YOU A CONFIDENT PERSON?

When you think of a confident person, what image comes to mind? Do you envision someone with a strong personality....someone who knows how to work a room full of people, easily striking up a conversation with anyone and everyone? Do you think of someone who sits down at a business meeting knowing exactly what they want and how they will get it, then execute their plan successfully? Do you think of a singer or a public speaker who feels more comfortable performing in front of a large audience than sitting with a friend in a coffee shop? Maybe you think of an athlete who is enormously talented and knows it....and has a swagger that intimidates opponents. Or perhaps you think of that person in your group of friends who joins a few of you for lunch and quickly dominates the conversation.

Two Types of Confidence

To be confident is to live boldly and without fear and to believe you will succeed. You can try to find confidence in yourself, or you can definitely find it in God. Before we go too far in your journey toward becoming your most confidence self, let me say that there are two kinds of confidence. The type of confidence you will have depends on) its source. One kind of confidence is the confidence people find in themselves that is rooted in their human strength, the force of their personality, and their natural abilities. Philippians 3:3 refers to this as confidence in the flesh," but we usually call it self-confidence," thinking this quality depends on a person's natural inner resources, People who are filled with self-confidence are quick to tell others about their own strong points and good qualities, believing they have produced those positive attributes in themselves. Instead of being grateful to God for their strengths, they take the credit for them.

The other type of confidence is also personal in nature, but it's rooted in dependence on God, not self. It comes from knowing God's love and acceptance, and from the humble realization that apart from Him, we can do nothing (John 15:5). I call this godly confidence or confidence in God because it draws its strength from the never-ending resources God offer us. People with this type of confidence are quick to recognize that the good things about them come from God, and they are thankful for the ways He has blessed them.

The apostle Paul understood the different between self-confidence and godly confidence. In Philippians 3 he mentions the reason he could have found confidence in himself. He actually says in Philippians 3:4: "If someone else thinks they have reasons to put confidence in the flesh, I have more," Then he lists some of his impressive credentials and accomplishments sense of strength and boldness you have within yourself but it does not come from anything you are doing, anything you have done, or anything you can do as a result of mere human strength. I often tell people that they can be confident even if they don't feel confident because it is based on faith, not feeling.

THE BEST KIND OF CONFIDENCE

When developing self-confidence, people place their trust in all kinds of things – their job, their spouse, their savings account, their knowledge or education, or their talents and abilities. The problem with putting confidence in any of these things that they subject to change, sometimes significantly and quickly. And if something can change, it is really not a good place to place your confidence.

I am convinced that the only place worthy of our confidence is in God. Unlike everything and everyone else, He is unshakeable. He never changes. He is "the same yesterday and today and forever" (Hebrews L3:8). Confidence in God is different from any other kind of confidence, and it is the deepest, strongest, longest lasting, best kind of confidence you can have.

What exactly is confidence in God? It is absolute trust in who God is....His character and His nature....and it is the confidence that comes from being in a personal relationship with Him. It is the deeply held conviction that He is trustworthy, that He will always make good on His promises, and that He has a wonderful plan for your life and wants to help you fulfill it. To be confident in Him means that you know beyond a shadow of a doubt that you can do anything you need to do in life through Christ who strengthens, you (Philippians 4:13) and that God works every situations in your life for your good because you love Him and are called according to His purpose (Romans 8:28). Confidence in God brings deep fulfillment and demands no striving at all. All you have to do is believe what His Word says about you and rest in those truths. Confidence in God doesn't call for self-effort; it depends on His grace.

YOU NEVER HAVE TO
LOSE CONFIDENCE IN GOD

You may remember the story of Nehemiah. This Jewish man, in exile in Persia, worked in the king's court and heard that the wall of Jerusalem had been broken down when the Babylonians destroyed the city and took the Jewish people into exile. He was so grieved about this that he asked the king's permission to go to Jerusalem and lead the effort to rebuild the wall. The king agreed.

Nehemiah and his helpers faced all kinds of opposition as they tried to reconstruct the wall, but they eventually finished it. When their enemies heard about this, according to Nehemiah 6:16, "all the surrounding nations were afraid and lost their self-confidence, because they realized that work had been done with the help of our God."

You can see from this story that it is possible, maybe even easy, to lose your self confidence. All it takes is a little fear or intimidation, or perhaps a mistake or a disappointment, and self confidence can vanish. This is because human strength is fickle. Sometimes you feel strong and sometimes you feel weak. But God never changes (Hebrews 13:8). He is always strong. Therefore, He will never fail you or be weak; you can trust Him at all times.

When you have confidence in God, you know that He is always there to help you, and you can live in freedom and boldness. You are open to learning new things and taking risks, because you know your confidence allows you to embrace life's opportunities boldly, eager to discover what awaits you. You know that every unknown is a chance to learn more about yourself, grow in God, and move toward fulfilling all the potential He place in you.

QUESTIONS TO HELP YOU

GROW IN CONFIDENCE

1. What is the difference between self-confidence and godly confidence?

2. In what specific area of your life do you need to grow in godly confidence? Ask God to help you develop that kind of trust and confidence as you read this book.

CONFIDENCE BOOSTERS

For we who worship by the Spirit of God....rely on what Christ Jesus has done for us. We put no confidence in human effort.

(Philippians 3:3 NLT)

We should not trust in ourselves but in God.

(2 Corinthians 1:9 KJV)

I am convinced and confident of this very thing, that He who has begun a good work in you will [continue to] perfect and complete it until the day of Christ Jesus.

(Philippians 1:6 AMP)

CHAPTER TWO

BOLD

Maybe you've stayed with me this far and you're still thinking Dr. Manning, I am a shy person, timid person....that's just my nature. I wouldn't even feel like myself if I acted confident and bold. I just don't think I can change. You may feel timid and shy, but you can choose to walk boldly through life. Your feelings don't have to determine your attitude, and it's time for a confident, courageous attitude. This doesn't mean becoming loud or aggressive. You can keep your sweet, reserved personality and still have a bold disposition on the inside.

The main truth I want you to remember is that you can feel afraid, timid, or downright cowardly and still decide to walk boldly....as though the fear does not exist. Fear can be present in all kinds of situations, but when you choose to ignore it, it has no power over you. As I have said often, "You can do it afraid."

Your free will (God-given ability to make choices) is stronger than your feelings if you will exercise it. Many people have catered to their feelings for so long that their emotions now control them. Perhaps you have allowed this to happen to you8. If so, the good news is that your will is like a muscle; it becomes weak if not exercised, but more you use it, the stronger it grows. As you begin to ask God to help you and exercise your willpower against your feelings, choosing to be brave instead of fearful, becoming the person you truly want to be....the one God designed and intends for you to be....will get easier and easier.

A WORD OF CAUTION

Some people are naturally outgoing or outspoken and may be considered bold, type A, or extroverted. People may refer to them as having a strong personality. These people have to overcome pride, bossiness, aggression, and false confidence. Like everyone, a type A person has strong points and also has tendencies that need to be worked on and overcome. Believe me, I know what I am talking about because I am that type A personality who loves to give direction and be in control. God has dealt very strongly with me about the foolishness of self-confidence and the wisdom of having my confidence in Him alone. The Book of Proverbs often refers to the fool as "the self-confidence fool."

The opposite of a type A person is the introvert, or someone who is shy, timid, and reserved. This kind of person needs to overcome shyness, timid, fear, the temptation to withdraw from challenges, and low confidence. I mention this because although this chapter focuses on boldness and I am sure about areas in which a naturally bold person may need to improve, I don't want to single out the extroverts. I want to point out that every personality type has areas that need improvement. That's the way God made us.

A bold person can often be assertive to the point of being rude. Sometimes, what people think is boldness is in reality, pride, which is something God's Word says that He hates (Proverbs 6:16-171.1 am a naturally bold person, and I have to stand against pride. It seems that bold people simply assume they are right about most things, and they don't mind telling other people just how right they are. While confidence is a good quality this kind of egotism is not true godly confidence. Thank God we can learn to have balance in our lives. We can benefit from our strength and overcome our weaknesses with His help. But we must lean on Him continually or we will backslide into old bad habits.

TRUE BOLDNESS DOESN'T IGNORE FEAR

Some people think they are bold, but they are mere rude, aggressive, and impudent. They would be much better off being honest and admitting that they are not as confident as they appear, but many of them struggle to do that. I must admit that I pretended to be brave for many years, even though I was filled with various kinds of fear. I thought that I was a bold man, but the truth is that

underneath the pretend I was very fearful and insure. I tried to convince myself.... and everyone around me....that I was not afraid of anything, which kept me from confronting my fears and dealing with them in a healthy way.

There is a difference between truly facing fear and simply ignoring it. When people pretend they are not afraid but they really are, they are not able to genuinely overcome their fears and develop true courage. They simply try to cover their fears with phony boldness.

When they do this, they are deceiving themselves and are off....putting to others. If they would simply be honest about the fact that they are afraid in certain ways, they could receive help and strength from God and others. People will always be better off humbly telling the truth and saying, "I feel fear, but I will move forward anyway."

HOW TRUE BOLDNESS HANDLES OFFENSE

Before I learned how to walk in true boldness, I was quick to speak my mind, but what I said was often foolish and inappropriate. I often took control of situations, thinking I would step out in boldness and do something since nobody else seemed to be doing anything, only to later realize that I had taken authority I should not have taken.

I frequently moved impatiently and too quickly, once again thinking I was bold, but I made many mistakes and hurt a lot of people because I did not take time to seek wisdom. I was really very immature and knew nothing about the kind of boldness and strength God can give.

If anyone offended or insulted me, I was quick to defend myself, by putting them in their place, and make it clear that I would not be mistreated. However, as I became a student of God's Word in an effort to grow spiritually by His grace, I learned, matured, and received correction and instruction from scriptures such as these:

> Fool show their annoyance at once, but the
> prudent overlook an insult.
>
> > (Proverbs 12:16)

> Do not take revenge, my dear friends, but leave
> Room for God s wrath, for it is written: "It is mine
> To avenge; I will repay," says the Lord.
>
> > (Romans 12:19)

Before I allowed God's Word to begin to change me, I was quick to let people know when they offended me and quick to try to vindicate myself. I thought I was bold, not realizing that genuinely bold, courageous people not only have the courage to take action but also demonstrate patience and wisdom, and they always trust that God will bring vengeance as needed in HIS TIMING AND His way

WHAT DOES TRUE BOLDNESS
LOOKS LIKE

A person who is genuinely bold and courageous is also humble. Some people think boldness and humility are mutually exclusive, but they are not. In fact, it's impossible to be truly bold without also being genuinely humble" Authentic confidence embodies both qualities.

Think about various people in the Bible who did great exploits, yet demonstrated great humility.

> Moses led God's people out of Egypt, yet he reached a point when his leadership had become too much for him, so his father in-law recommended delegating certain tasks to others. (Exodus 18:13-26)

> Mary, the mother of Jesus, was given the greatest honor on earth....to bring God's Son into the world. When the angel Gabriel announced God's plan to her, she acknowledged that the Lord had been mindful of the humble state of his servant." (Luke 1:48)

> The apostle Paul traveled extensively, zealously spreading the gospel, and he wrote books of the Bible that we still live by today, yet he called himself the worse of sinners. (1 Timothy 1:15)

These people and others throughout the Bible viewed themselves through the lens of humility. They knew their flaws, but they did not let their shortcomings cause them to back away from God's plan for their lives. They were humble enough to realize that they were nothing apart from God, yet bold enough to say yes when He wanted to use them.

I pray that you will develop true boldness and confidence in your life and that you will walk in humility while also boldly following God, no matter what He calls you to do. Remember that true boldness demonstrates courage in the face of fear....not the absence of fear. Boldness requires wisdom, patience, and faith.... not in your human strength, but in all that God can do through you.

QUESTIONS TO HELP YOU

GROW IN CONFIDENCE

1. Why is facing fear so much better than ignoring it while pretending to be brave?

2. How has your perspective of boldness changed after reading this chapter? Ask God to give you a confident but humble heart.

CONFIDENCE BOOSTER

When I called, you answered me; you greatly emboldened me. (Psalm 138:3)

Though an army besiege me, my heart will not fear, though war break out against me, even then I will be confident. (Psalm 27:3)

After they prayed....they were all filled with the Holy Spirit and spoke the word of God boldly. (Acts 4:31)

CHAPTER THREE
NO COMPARISON

And important key to becoming confidently you is understanding and embracing yourself uniqueness and accepting yourself. You accept your strengths and weaknesses your success and your mistakes, your good points and your not-so good points. You do not allow yourself to fall into self-hatred, but you embrace every unique quality that makes you who you are. This does not mean you never try to improve in appropriate ways, because God has given us the Holy Spirit to lead us into all truth and to help us become more like Jesus, but you do not need to compare yourself to others and then try to be like they are or compete with them in an effort to be the very best in every area of your life.

I do not believe it is possible for anyone to be confident as long as they compare themselves to others. Comparison is a waste of time and energy, which would be better invested in making the most of who God created you to be and enjoying that. He does not compare you with other people; He knows everything about you and loves you unconditionally, accepting you the way you are, so why should you compare yourself with anyone else? Your weaknesses are not a surprise to God. He knew all about each one of them long before you discovered them, and He will chose you to be His special child.

While comparison does not serve people well, many people still struggle with it. If you are one of them, I believe this chapter will help you break free from the frustration of comparing yourself with someone else and enable you to live with boldness and confidence, enjoying the person God made you to be. You can enjoy your talents, abilities, and personality without comparing yourself to anyone else. Your uniqueness is what makes you special.

RESIST THE WORLD'S WAY

We live in a world that pushes us to compare ourselves with others and compete with them in terms of how we look, what we accomplish, how much we own, where we live, and even how "successful" our spouses or children are. In our society, certain things are considered better that others, and each day we see images or advertisements that push us to be or have the "best." God wants us to be our best for His glory, but we don't need to be like someone else in order to do that.

Sadly, some people spend time, energy, and money they do not have pursuing what the world says they should have or achieve. Then, once they achieve it, it has been replaced with something people view as more desirable. I remember when people were happy to have any kind of phone in their house, but now even mobile phone have a hierarchy. Companies offer new models often, and people feel the need to upgrade, even if the phone they have works well and meets their needs.

Much advertising is geared to prod people to think they are somehow less than others if they do not look better or have more than those around them. We are bombarded with messages: If you wear this brand of clothes, people will know you are successful!

If you use this face cream, you will look much younger than you really are! If you try this new diet and lose those few extra pounds, you will be more attractive and accepted! The world consistently gives us the impression that we need to be something other than what we are and that we need some product, program, or prescription can help us do it. There is nothing wrong with wanting to look our best or have nice things, but our motive for doing so should not be to keep up with someone else or look better than they do.

The fact is, no matter how good we look, how talented or smart we are, or how much success we achieve, somebody somewhere will look better, be smarter, or achieve more....and then we have to decide whether we want to compare and compete all over again. Always struggling to maintain the number one position is hard work. In fact, it's exhausting.

One of the Ten Commandments is "You shall not covet" (Exodus 20:17). This means we are not to lust after what other people have, how they look, their talents, their personality, or anything else about them. Jesus found His disciples arguing over which of them was the greatest, and He said the greatest among you is the one who serves (Matthew 20:26-271. Only a confident person can serve others and do so with joy.

I believe confidence is found in doing the best we can with what we have to work with and not in comparing or competing with other people. In fact, when we have confidence, we never feel the need to compare or compete with anyone. We are never truly free until we no longer have a need to impress anyone. Real fulfillment and satisfaction come not from comparing ourselves to others, but in being our personal best.

DECIDE NOT TO COMPARE
YOURSELF WITH OTHERS

For years, I struggled trying to be like my friends, and other people. I seemed to find myself constantly comparing myself with someone else and in the process rejecting and disapproving of the person God created me to be. After years of misery, I finally understood that God does not make mistakes; He intentionally makes all of us different, and different is not bad. The fact that everyone is different simply showcases God's creativity and the interesting variety He is capable of displaying.

The Bible teaches us that God intricately forms each of us in our mother's womb with His own hand and that He writes all of our days in His book before any of them take shape (Psalm 139:13,16). As I said, God does not make mistakes, so we should accept ourselves as God's creation and let Him help us be the unique, precious individuals that He intends for us to be.

Confidence begins with self-acceptance, which is made possible through a strong faith in God's love and plan for our lives. I truly believe that we insult God, our Maker, when we compare ourselves with others and desire to be what they are. Let me encourage you to make the decision that you will never again compare yourself with someone else. Appreciate others for who they are and enjoy the wonderful person you are.

I often say that confidence is all about focusing on what you can do and not worrying about what you can't do. Some people works hard to improve in their areas of weakness that they neglect or overlook their strengths. Confidence people do not concentrate on their weaknesses; they maximize their strengths. When we are busy making the most of our strengths, we no longer have time or desire to compare ourselves with others.

QUESTIONS TO HELP YOU

GROW IN CONFIDENCE

1. In what areas do you struggle most with comparison?
   Look? Possessions? Intellect? Talents and abilities?
   Accomplishments? Education? Others?

2. Think about your strengths for a moment. List as many of your best qualities as you can think of here. They may not be things you can do, but personality traits such as kindness, discipline, or being a dependable friend.

CONFIDENCE BOOSTERS

Now you {collectively} are Christ's body, and individually {you are} members of it {each with his own special purpose and function}. (1 Corinthians 12:27)

We do not dare to classify or compare ourselves with some who commend themselves. When they measure themselves by themselves and compare themselves with themselves, they are not wise. (2 Corinthians 10:12)

CHAPTER FOUR

BE YOURSELF

One of the many benefits of confidence is that it empowers us to live authentically. We can be exactly who we are exactly as God created us to be, in all of our specialness and uniqueness....with no regrets, and no apologies. What a free and happy way to live I When we have confidence, we never feel the need to compare or compete with anyone. Being confident also means we don't have to pretend to be somebody we aren't in order to feel good about ourselves in relation to other people, because we are secure in who we are even if we're different from those around us.

I believe that confidence gives us permission to be different, to be unique. God has created every person in a unique way, yet many people spend their lives trying to be like someone else....and feeling miserable as a result. Trust me, you can be sure of this: God will never help you be anyone but yourself. He wants you to be you.

NO MORE PRETENDING TO BE
SOMEONE ELSE

The primary reason many people pretend to be someone they are not is that they want to please other people. Wanting to please is common desire, and in itself it is not negative or wrong is some ways. But many times people find that they simply cannot be what others want them to be, so they make a big mistake by deciding to pretend so that others will accept them or think highly of them. Them try to "fake it" til they make it.

Faking it, or pretending to be someone or something, you are not, is being untrue to yourself, which is something you should never do.

Jesus did not appreciate the hypocrites or phonies in His days, so you can be sure that He does not want you to or me to pretend either. Even if the person you are right now is who you want to be or know you should be, at least be real. You will grow and change over time, but God loves and accept yourself too.

Don't spend your life pretending that you like things you don't like, or frequently being with people you don't enjoy and pretending you do. To some people, this might sound very "un-Christian," but it really isn't. Jesus told us to love everyone, but He did not say we had to love being with everyone. Some people are more compatible with us than others, and that is okay. There are people that simply we don't fit in with....and people we do. Our personalities don't blend or work well together with everyone else's personalities, and we can grow frustrated or exhausted pretending to like people who are not a good fit or match for us. We can ask God to help us behave properly when we need to be together, but trying to be in close working relationship or trying to force a friendship day in and day out-pretending to enjoy it when we don't is not beneficial for anyone.

We should love everyone and be willing to help them if they have a need. We should not say unkind things about anyone or critically judge them. We should show other people respect and realize they are valuable to God. But we don't necessarily need to spend a lot of time with people if we don't have interests or simply don't blend well together.

Sadly, the world is full of pretender. People pretend to be happy when they are miserable, and they try to do jobs that are way over their heads because they feel they should do them in order to be admired or to maintain a certain reputation. People have many masks and can become quite adept at changing them as circumstances require.

I believe that not being true to yourself is one of the biggest confidence thieves that exists. People can pretend to be confident, and perhaps others fall for the charade, but deep down inside, pretender know they are faking it. "To be true to yourself in a world that is constantly trying to make you something else is the greatest accomplishment." Be yourself, and you'll find confidence.

HAVE FRIENDS WHO GIVE YOU SPACE TO BE YOURSELF

Some people seem to prefer being around us if we pretend or put on a false personality that appeals to them, but there are those rare individuals who actually encourage individuality and value us just the way we are. Spending time with those who accept and affirm us increases our confidence and our enjoyment of life.

One of the many qualities I have appreciated about my little sister, Patricia Guillory, over the years is that she gives me space and even encourages me to be myself. For example, I am a person who like to travel. When I know I need to get away from certain people. I am very grated that my little sister Patricia Guillory so graciously accommodates my need to get away from certain people. I have met a lot of couples who were offended when one or the other had this need or felt personally rejected because of it. The truth is, to nurture healthy relationships, we must give people the space and freedom they need. Having someone in your life who is secure enough to encourage you to be who you are and help you celebrate your uniqueness and individual needs is wonderful. Nobody wants to be made to feel as though something is wrong with them because they want to do something other than what everyone else is doing or want you to do.

Of course, if we want to be encouraged in our own individual unlike independence, we must sow the same type of freedom and respect into other people's lives. We should realize that they have their own needs and desires, and that they may need to pursue certain interests apart from us or spend time alone, as I have needed to do. When we support their expressions of uniqueness, we

give them confidence, and we feel confident too. This remind me to acknowledge someone that I met in Redding, CA, and the person I'm talking about is name Richard Kuilmber, he also encourage me to follow my dreams and never to give up on pursuing it. If we know that our relationship is solid, and we are secure enough to allow others to grow and do what they need to do, just as they allow us to fulfill the needs that we have.

ENJOY THE RIDE

Occasionally people say they are not sure who they really are. Perhaps they have spent so many years trying to be like someone else that they have lost themselves. If this describes you let me encourage you to begin now purposefully discovering and expressing who you really are. If you have spent years having to fulfill responsibility that have not allowed you the freedom to find out who you are and express yourself without reservation, this may take time, but it can be a wonderful adventure. Don't be discouraged if it takes a while; just enjoy the ride. yYu will find great freedom and joy in being yourself. If you'd like to discover more about who you really are and how to experience the joy of being yourself, I believe you would find this book helpful.

QUESTIONS TO HELP YOU

GROW IN CONFIDENCE

1. What is stressful about pretending? How can you avoid being trapped by it.

2. Why is being your true, authentic self so important?

CONFIDENCE BOOSTER

I praise you because I am fearful and wonderfully made; your works are wonderful, I know that fully well. (Psalm 139:14)

Am I now trying to win the approval of human beings, or of God? Or am I trying to please people? If I were still trying to please people, I would not be a servant of Christ. (Galatians 1:10)

The Lord does not look at the things people look at. People look at the outward appearance, but the Lord looks at the heart. (1 Samuel 16:7)

CHAPTER FIVE

STAND UP FOR YOURSELF

Stand up to your obstacles and do something
about them. You will find they haven't half the
strength you think they do.

Becoming your most confident self involves learning to stand up for yourself
and developing what I call "balance independence. This means being able to
trust and depend on God and other people in healthy, appropriate ways, yet also
establishing your own individual identity....a strong sense of who you are and
what you can do for yourself without needing other people's approval. Don't lose
the power that God has given you to be an individual.

John 15:5 says that we can do nothing apart from God. And Philippians 4:13 says,
"l can do all things through Christ who strengths me." (NKJV) When we consider
Philippians 4:13 and John 15:5 together, we see that without Christ, we are nothing
and we can do nothing. But with Him, we are everything He wants us to be, we have
everything He intends for us to have, and we can do everything He calls us to do.
Because this is true, we can be confident and we can live in balance independence.

When we recognize our need for God and our total dependence on Him as
well is our need for healthy human relationship we gain the balance we need
in order to become dependent in appropriate ways. This included fulfilling our
responsibilities and taking care of ourselves physical, financially, emotionally,
spiritually. It also includes being able stand up for ourselves by having our own
opinions, learning to say no and to set appropriate boundaries when necessary,
and dealing with criticism. Let's look at each of these individually.

YOUR OWN OPINIONS

Opinions are not truths or facts; they are viewpoints, beliefs, or perspectives. According to the Merriam-Webster.com Dictionary, an opinion is "a view, judgment, or appraisal formed in the mind about a particular matter." Simply put, your opinion is what you think about something.

People opinions vary greatly, and every person has a right to think as they choose. It is important for you to develop your own opinion on certain matters and not allow other people or public opinion to influence you to change it unless you have good reason to do so. Sometimes we change our opinion because we have heard and considered someone else's viewpoint, and it good to be able to do so. Or, over time, you may change your opinions, but they will hopefully evolve as a result of gaining new insights, perspectives, or information.... not because other people pressure you to change your mind.

Confident people know what they believe and why they believe it, and they are comfortable expressing their opinions graciously, kindly, and respectfully. When others disagree with them, they are not intimidated. They do not attempt to change anyone else's mind, but they don't let anyone change their mind either.

You are entitled to your opinion, but that doesn't mean you should always share it. Be wise enough to know when to talk about it and when to keep quiet.

The Bible says that Jesus "knew that the Father had put all things under his power, and that he had come from God and was returning to God," put on a towel and washed the disciples' feet (John 13:3-5). The Amplified Bible, Classic Edition version of this scripture indicates that He put on a "servant's" towel. He was able to do this seemingly lowly task because He knew who He was and had no need to impress anyone. He was truly the greatest among them, and He was the ultimate servant.

SAY NO WHEN NECESSARY

Another way to stand up for yourself is to say no when it is the wise course of action for you. Anyone who says yes to everyone all the time is headed for trouble. When people want you to do something they won't be happy if you tell them no, but sooner or later you must decide if you will spend your time and energy making other people happy or if you will pursue happiness for yourself within God's will.

A confident person can say no when they need to. They can endure people's displeasure and understand that if they disappoint someone who truly wants a relationship with them, that person will ultimately want them to be free to make their own decisions. In healthy relationships, both parties encourage each other to follow the guidance of the Holy Spirit and say no when needed, and they will support each other in doing so.

Sometimes you have to say no to other people in order to say yes to yourself. Otherwise you will end up bitter and resentful, feeling that somewhere in the process of trying to keep others happy you lost yourself. You may have a desire to please people, especially close friends or family members, but it is important to be led by God and stay balance in this area. Always remember that you are valuable and that you to do things you want to do as well as doing things for others.

If you are like most people, you may have tendency to want to explain yourself when you say no to someone. Perhaps you think they will accept the no better if you have a good reason for saying it. But there are also times when you cannot explain why you had to say no. You may say no because you don't have God's peace about saying yes, and you don't know why. There is a reason, but God may not reveal it until later.

People often want us to justify our decisions, but we can resist that temptation. We simply need to be led by God's Spirit (another way of saying this is to say we need to follow our hearts) when deciding to say yes or no to requests, opportunities, or commitments. This is what I have to learned to do. Sometimes I don't fully understand why I don't feel something isn't right for me, but I have to learned that if I do feel that way, I should not go against my own conscience in order to make someone happy. I often say, "I just don't have peace about it" or "I don't feel right about it." Mature people will respect your no, even when you do not know how to explain it.

COPING WITH CRITICISM

The third way you stand up for yourself is to learn to cope with criticism. Life seems to be full of critics, and no matter what you do, someone may speak negatively about you. Criticism is difficult for most of us to hear, and one critical remark can damage a person's self-image. For this reason, it is important to learn to deal with criticism and not let it bother you.

I encourage you to know yourself, know what's in your heart, have your own opinions, and not let criticism cause you to sway from them. People may judge you, but can choose not to let their judgment affect you. You may or may not choose to respond to the criticism with words or actions, but you can always handle it in your heart by refusing to believe it while choosing to forgive the person who criticized you. Always ask God if the one criticized you is right, because it is important to be teachable and make appropriate adjustments. But don't become offended or angry and give the devil a foothold in your life.

Sometimes people who are criticized the most are the ones who work hardest to do something constructive with their lives. I am amazed when people who do nothing want to criticize those who try to do something.

I may not always do everything right, but at least I am attempting to do something to make the world a better place and to help hurting people. I believe that this is pleasing to God. After many years of suffering because of criticisms and trying to gain people's approval. I finally decided that if God is happy with me, that is enough. I hope that will always be enough for you too.

Learning to stand up for yourself is necessary for becoming a truly confident person. You can do this by living with balance independence, developing your own opinions and sticking with them unless God leads you to change them, saying no when you need to say no, and learning to deal with criticism. God has made you special and unique. No one has a right to try to change your mind about that or to criticize who He has made you to be or what He had called you to do.

QUESTIONS TO HELP YOU

GROW IN CONFIDENCE

1. What do you need to say no to in your life?
   What do you need to say yes to?

2. What can you do to stay balanced when others criticize you, or when their opinions difference from yours?

CONFIDENCE BOOSTER

Be on your guard; stand firm in the faith; be courageous, be strong.

(1 Corinthians 16:13)

Do not judge, or you too will be judged. For in the same way you judge others, you will be judged, and with the measure you use, it will be measure to you.

(Matthew 7:1-2)

Therefore, there is now no condemnation for those who are in Christ Jesus.

(Romans 8:1)

CHAPTER SIX

STAY POSITIVE

Never yield to gloomy anticipation.
Place your hope and confidence in God.
He has no record of failure.

A positive attitude is a necessary and defining quality of a confident person. Confident people think positive thoughts, speak positive words, and have a positive expectation for everything they do. They know that confidence and negativity are like oil and water and simply do not mix.

I was once a very negative person. But thank God I finally learned that being positive is much more fulfilling and fruitful, and it is the will of God. I have learned to choose to be positive ever since. We all have a choice: we can be negative or we can be positive. Furthermore I am "allergic" to negative people! This decision determines how we think, speak, and act. We make the choice, and then we become either positive or negative people by building positive or negative habits though repetitions behavior. Looking on the bright side of life is just as easy as looking on the dark side. Why not believe something good will happen instead of presuming things will turn out bad.

If you struggle with negativity, your background may be similar to mine. I grew up in a negative atmosphere around negative people. They were my role models, and I learned to think and act as they did. I did not realize my negative attitude was a problem until I got older, and on my own. people that was positive about everything began asking me why were I so negative? As I started thinking about it, I realize that I had always been that way. No wonder my life was so negative! I began to understand that I never expected anything good....so I never got it. All my negativity got me was jail and prison. Being negative led to many, problems and disappointments in my life, which further fueled my negativity. It took time for me to change, but I am convinced that if I can change, anyone can. This is why now I am "allergic" to negative people.

I believe one of the biggest reasons people resist thinking positively is that they have convinced themselves that if they do not expect anything good to happen, they will not be disappointed if it doesn't. This is a sad way to live, and people who think this way are mistaken. This kind of thinking actually cause them to live in disappointment. Every day is filled with disappointment for a person whose thoughts and expectations are negative. But for those who think positively and expect positive outcomes, every day is filled with hope and joy. This does not mean that nothing disappointing ever happens.

Disappointments come alone for everyone, but not as often for those who think positively. When disappointments do happen, a positive attitude enables people to deal with them better than a negative one. Keep in mind that if you have lived with a negative attitude and negative circumstances for a long time, it will take time to turn it around. Don't have unrealistic expectations. Things will change, but you need to give your new positive attitude time to turn negative circumstance around.

POSITIVITY IS GOD'S REALITY

Some people say that they resist thinking positively because "that's not reality." But the truth is that positive thinking can change your current reality. God is optimistic all the time; positivity is His reality. It is the way He is, the way He think, and the way He encourages us to be. According to Romans 8:28, "In all things God works for the good of those who love him, who have been called according to his purpose."

A common static tells us 90 percent of what we worry about never happens. This makes me wonder why people assume that being negative is more realistic than being positive. We simply need to choose whether we want to look at things from God' perspective or not.

People often want us to justify our decisions, but we can resist that temptation. We simply need to be led by God's Spirit (another way of saying this is to say we need to follow our hearts) when deciding to say yes or no to requests, opportunities, or commitments. This is what I have to learned to do. Sometimes I don't fully understand why I don't feel something isn't right for me, but I have to learned that if I do feel that way, I should not go against my own conscience in order to make someone happy. I often say, "I just don't have peace about it" or "l don't feel right about it." Mature people will respect your no, even when you do not know how to explain it.

COPING WITH CRITICISM

The third way you stand up for yourself is to learn to cope with criticism. Life seems to be full of critics, and no matter what you do, someone may speak negatively about you. Criticism is difficult for most of us to hear, and one critical remark can damage a person's self-image. For this reason, it is important to learn to deal with criticism and not let it bother you.

I encourage you to know yourself, know what's in your heart, have your own opinions, and not let criticism cause you to sway from them. People may judge you, but can choose not to let their judgment affect you. You may or may not choose to respond to the criticism with words or actions, but you can always handle it in your heart by refusing to believe it while choosing to forgive the person who criticized you. Always ask God if the one criticized you is right, because it is important to be teachable and make appropriate adjustments. But don't become offended or angry and give the devil a foothold in your life.

Keep in mind that the devil lies to us and tells us that our circumstances will be bad. He then temps us to think accordingly, so we must be able to recognize what he is doing and resist it immediately.

Since God is positive and the devil is negative, let me ask you: Who is doing your thinking for you? Have you renewed your mind according to God's Word (Romans 72:21, so you can think as He think? Are you choosing your thoughts carefully so they are positive and in agreement with His Word? Or do you allow the enemy to influence your thinking? The enemy wants you to think negatively prevents you from being aggressive, bold, and confident in healthy ways. Why not think positive and live confidently.

STAYING POSITIVE THOUGH SETBACKS

Being positive is easy as long as everything is going good for you. But when circumstances turn negative because you face disappointments or make mistakes, that's when you'll need to make an extra effort to stay positive.

Setbacks are not failures. You are never a failure because you try some things that do not work out. The only way to fail is to stop trying. Instead of allowing mistakes to stop you, let them teach and train you. I say that if I try something and it does not work, at lease I know not to do it again.

Many people are confused about what to do with their lives. They don't know that God's will is for them; they are without direction. I once felt the same way, but I discovered my destiny by trying several things. When l tried writing a book teaching God's Word I found where I fit in. I could have spent my life confused, but I thank God that I was confident enough to step out on faith and discover what was right for me.

If you are doing nothing with your life because you are not sure what to do, pray and begin trying something different things. God will lead you to something that is a perfect fit for you.

Think of it this way. When you go out to buy a new outfit, you may try on several pieces of clothing until you find what fit right, feels comfortable, and looks good on you. Why not use this same approach while discovering your destiny? Obviously, there are some things you cannot just "try"....such as being an astronaut or professional dancer....but one thing is for sure: You cannot drive a parked car. Get your life moving in some direction.

I am not suggesting going into debt to find out if you should own a business, but you could begin in some small way and, if it works, take it to the next level. As you take steps of faith, your destiny will unfold. God will make His will clear to you. Look for open doors in your life, because this is one way that God speaks to people. He opens right doors and close wrong ones. A confident person is not afraid to make mistakes, and if they do they recover and press on.

God always provides new beginnings. His mercies are new every day or morning (Lamentations 3:22-23). Jesus chose disciples who had weakness and made mistakes, but He worked with them and helped them become all that they could be. He will do the same for you, if you will let Him. Let go of what lies behind you and press toward the things ahead (Philippines 3:13). Be confident and optimistic about the future instead of staying stuck in your past.

Recovering from pain or disappointment is a choice....decision to let go and move forward. Gather up the fragments of your mistakes and give them to Jesus, and He will make sure that nothing is wasted (John 6:12). Refuse to dwell on what you have lost, and begin looking for opportunities to use what you still have.

Not only can you recover from your setbacks, but God can also use you to help other people recover from theirs. Be a living example of a confident person who always bounces back, no matter how difficult or frequent the setbacks may be. Don't ever say, "I just cannot go on." Instead say, "I can do whatever I need to do through Christ who strengthens me. I will never quit, because God is on my side. Knowing that God is with you and that He is for you will help keep you positive and confident in every situations.

QUESTIONS TO HELP YOU

GROW IN CONFIDENCE

1. In what areas of your life are you tempted to think negatively. How can you change your thinking so you can be positive instead?

2. Think of someone....maybe someone you know or someone you have read about.... Who has overcome many setbacks with God's help. How does this person inspire you to deal with challenges?

CONFIDENCE BOOSTER

I can do all things through Christ who strengthen me.

(Philippians 4:13)

"For I know the plans I have for you," declares the Lord, plans to prosper you and not to harm you, plans to give you hope and a future.

(Jeremiah 29:11)

CHAPTER SEVEN

SPEAK WITH CONFIDENCE

According to Matthew L2:34, whatever is in your heart comes out of your mouth, through your words. And what you say with your mouth affects your heart. Thoughts and words flow in a cycle, and people often wonder which comes first. It really doesn't matter because they affect each other, and as you learned in the previous chapter, both your thoughts and your words need to be positive in order for you to most confidently person. In this chapter, I want to focus specifically on

the power of words because you can truly change your life with the words you speak.

Consider this amazing truth in Proverbs 18:21: "The tongue has power of life and death, and those who love it will eat its fruit." According to this verse, the power of life and death is in the words we speak, and we often have to eat them, meaning to be accountable for them. For the tongue to have "the power of life and death" means that our words can be positive, uplifting, encouraging, and helpful in a situation, or they can be negative, discouraging, and detrimental.

BE CAUTIOUS WITH YOUR WORDS

Until we realize how powerful our words are, we may use them carelessly and pay little attention to what we say. Think about it: How often do you casually say things you would not say if you thought they would actually happen, such as .This situation make me sick, "I am sick and tired of this," or "This is driving me crazy?" I understand that these are figures of speech or common ways of conveying strong feelings in certain situations, and these are a few examples of many. But really, who wants to be sick, or sick and tired, or crazy? I'm sure you see my point. We often say things we don't really mean and would never want to happen.

This brings me to a specific phase I believe we should be diligent about not using if we want to grow in confidence. People say it often without even realizing what they are saying. How many times have you said or heard I'm afraid....

For example:

- "I'm afraid I will never lose weight."
- My company has been sold, and I'm afraid the new owner will let me go."
- "I'm afraid my kids will get in trouble."
- "I'm afraid it's going to rain."
- "I'm afraid the refrigerator is about to go out."

If we heard a recording of every time we have said "I'm afraid," we would probably be amazed that our lives are going as well as they are.

If we really understood the power in our words, I think we would change the way we talk. Our talk should be confident and bold, not fearful. Fearful talk not only affects us in adverse ways, but it can also have a negative impact on the people around us. If you are a parent, for example, and your children frequently hear you say that you are afraid, over time, will that inspire them to be confident, or will it encourage them to be anxious and fearful?

I want to make a bold statement right now: If you will simply change the way you talk and stop casually saying you are afraid, you will begin to feel stronger, bolder, more courageous, and less afraid.

James 3:8 says, "No human being can tame the tongues." I believe this means that we cannot discipline our words without God's help. We are accustomed to speaking certain words without paying attention to them that we definitely need God's help simply to recognize fearful, negative, foolish, silly, and sinful talk.

Even after we recognize the need to be more careful about our speech, we still need to act on that realization and develop new habits in our speech. Forming new habits takes time, so don't get discouraged with yourself if it happens slowly. Keep at it, and little by litter, you will develop the habit of saying things that add to your life, not take away from it.

SPEAK LIFE TO YOURSELF

The best way I know to be sure you are speaking life to yourself is to speak in agreement with God's Word and speak it aloud. Don't talk about yourself according to the way you feel, think, or look. Speak what God says over your life; don't say about yourself what others say unless what they say agree with what God says.

Perhaps your parents, teachers, or friends spoke to you in a way that caused you to lack confidence. They may not have intended to harm you, but their words had a negative impact. I want you to know those words do not have to influence you anymore. You can declare that those old words are not true and that they have no power over you. You can also change the words you speak about yourself, which will change your image of yourself.

Even if you had a longtime habit of speaking negatively about yourself, you can change, starting today. Resist the urge to make comments such as "I just don't have any confidence, or "I'll never overcome my fears." Anything God says you can have, as long as you are in agreement with Him.

I'm sure you get the idea, and now you can find many scriptures to speak aloud and apply to your life. To get started, you might consider using the one at the end of each chapter of this book.

As you speak God's Word aloud, you renew your mind, meaning that you can change the way you think and feel about yourself (Romans 12:2) Stop saying "I'm depressed and discouraged," "I'm really to give up" or "Nothing good ever happens to me." This kind of talk is self-defeating. Words such as these cannot add to your life, but they can certainly prevent you from enjoying it.

If you have considered yourself a person with low self-esteem or low confidence, who is shy and fearful, I believe today can be a turning point for you. However, you will have to be persistent. Speak God's Word again and again. Let it renew your mind more and more. God's Word always has power in it, and when you believe it and speak it consistently, it will change your life.

When you speak consistently, it influences the people around you. When you sound confident in yourself, they will be confident in you also. Don't be arrogant, but do be confident. Start talking and walking with confidence, and expect wonderful things to happen in your life.

QUESTIONS TO HELP YOU

GROW IN CONFIDENCE

1. Ask God to help you pay attention to your words and notice how many times you say the word afraid (or any negative word). What can you do to change your speech to be more positive and confident?

2. What are several examples of life-giving words you will begin to speak over yourself? Say these words every time you are tempted to speak negative words.

CONFIDENCE BOOSTER

Set a guard over my mouth, Lord; keep watch over the door of my life.

(Psalm 141:3)

The one who has knowledge uses words with restraint, and whoever has understanding is even-tempered.

(Proverbs 17:27)

Words from the mouth of the wise are gracious, but fools are consumed by their own lips.

(Ecclesiastes 10:12)

CHAPTER EIGHT

CONFIDENT PEOPLE TAKE ACTION

A humble man is not afraid of failure
in fact, he is not afraid of anything.

Confident people are people of action. They do not sit around and wait for good things to happen; they prayed fully move forward, doing what they know to do and trusting God to guide them to their next steps. Some people, though, hesitate to move forward for various reasons, and their lives come to a standstill. They become stagnant. When this happens, they do not enjoy their lives, they don't do anything to benefit others, and they do not fulfill the purpose for which they were

created for. Everyone can have a slow day once in a while, but when a confident person sees that their life has reached the point of stagnation, they shake it off and get moving in a positive direction.

When a puddle of water is stagnant, the water does not circulate, and fresh water has no way to get into it. The water simply sits. Over time, if the sun doesn't evaporate it first, bacteria can thrive and the water can turn green. The water can actually become unhealthy.

People can become stagnant too, Stagnant can happen to anyone at any time, and it happens a little bit at a time, and it is almost imperceptible. When we stop experiencing and expressing joy, when we no longer want to take risks, when our dreams and visions for our life grow dim, when life seems boring and we feel predictable, when our creativity wanes, or when we feel we have so many problems that we can't do anything productive-these are good signs stagnation has set in.

Stagnation is an enemy of confidence, because where stagnation is, lethargy, despair, discouragement, and even depression can follow.

Stagnation takes place for many reasons....stress, laziness, becoming too busy, increased responsibilities, or simply losing interest in activities that were once exciting and fun. One of the major causes of stagnation is fear. People often refuse to move forward because they are afraid they will make a mistake, afraid they will fail, afraid others will ridicule or reject them, afraid their friends and families won't understand and support them. Or they may be afraid they will be out of God's will, or perhaps they are afraid of all the unknowing that lie ahead of them if they take a confident step of faith. They are so afraid of the negative possibilities involved in moving forward that they do not even consider the positive potential of stepping out and try something. Confidence is the opposite of fear, and that's why confident people do all they can do to avoid stagnation.

HOW TO STAND AGAINST STAGATION

I believe everyone will stagnate if they don't actively resist it. It is easy to just float along with everyone else doing the same thing every day. Only rare individuals are willing to swim upstream when drifting downstream with everyone else would be so easy. One of the most valuable lessons I have learned in my life is that there are many things I must do "on purpose." I can't wait to feel like doing them, and sometimes my flesh does not want to do them, but I do them anyway. This is one way I stand against stagnation and keep my confidence level high. For example, I deliberately take care of my res possibilities, because I know it is very important. Even though they don't show any kind of appreciation, I do it anyway. I also encourage others, especially the youngest that's try to cover up their problems using drugs.

This is out the ordinary for me but I intentionally do it on purpose. I also spend time every day in prayer and fellowship with God because I want to honor Him and always give Him His rightful place in my life, which is first place.

Whatever it takes for you to keep your life interesting, do it on purpose. If you do this intentionally, it will make a big difference in your quality of life. Don't just put in your time here on earth, instead enjoy your life and make the world glad that you are here. You can't do that if you sit around like a puddle of water, so resist stagnation and keep your life fresh, vibrant, and confident. Stop using excuses to keep you from doing something out of the ordinary, and step out on confidence faith. Do it on purpose!

YOU WERE CREATED TO
BE PRODUCTIVE

Many times, people feel stagnant and they want do anything, and they don't do what they long to do because they are afraid. Before I go any further, I want to pause for a moment to say this:

> Matthew 10:26 says, "So have no fear" so why are people afraid, God didn't put the spirit of fear in us. Also we are justified by faith. I want to encourage you to stop saying "I'm afraid." And step out on faith and do something out of the ordinary on purpose. Remember we are justified by faith not fear.

Now back to the lesson: Some people are actually so afraid to do something that they form a habit of doing nothing. They sit idly by and become jealous of the people have the life they would like to have. They become resentful because things never workout for them. They fail to realize that things cannot workout for them if they don't at lease make an effort to do something.

Productivity is good for all of us. As matter of fact, God said we should work six days and rest one. (Exodus 31:15). That's what He did when He created the world (Genesis 2:2), and it shows how important work, to be enjoy the life He has given us, and to make a difference in the world, not to sit idly by doing nothing.

I know a woman who has allowed herself to become very passive due to some pain and disappointment in her life. I recently asked her had she answer the letter you received back and she answer, "I just don't have time or the motivation to do it." She is allowing her feelings and the devil lies to control her decisions instead of resisting it, and doing what she knows she should do. This woman is a beautiful person and has a good heart, but as long as she goes for the devil lies and her passive attitude it's going to rule her life and will never be productive.

If you feel your confidence is a bit low right now, may I suggest that you just do something out of the ordinary, and refuse to live in stagnation. Find a way to get up and get going in a direction that makes you happy and help you feel you are special and a productive person. There are several good stories in the Bible about people who were not doing anything due to illness or infirmity. In a number of those situations, they asked Jesus for help, and He simply told them to "get up."

One well-known Bible story of someone who needed to get up is the story of the man at the pool of Bethesda. He was an invalid, and he knew that if he could be the first person into the pool when the water was stirred, he would be healed, but he lay there year after year, waiting for someone to help him into the pool.

Then one day, Jesus went to the pool and saw this man lying on his mat, as usual, and learned that he had been there for thirty-eight years. He asked the man a very important question:" Do you want to get well?" (John 5:6).

The man answered: "I have no one to help me into the pool when the water is stirred. While I am trying to get in, someone else goes down ahead of me"

(John 5:7). Jesus responded immediately: "Get up! Pick up your mat and walk" (John 5:8). The man was cured instantly, and he started walking.

For thirty- eight years, that man had felt sorry for himself so he just lay there and did nothing. The answer to his problem surfaced when he made an effort to move. You may think you are waiting on God, but maybe He is waiting for you to simply "move."

A lack of confidence will keep you still and stagnant, lying on your mat, so to speak. But an attitude of faith and a willingness to get up and do something productive will cause you to feel confident again. And the more confident you are, the more productive, the more fulfilling, and the happier you will be. I believe that if we do what we can do, God will do what we cannot do.

QUESTIONS TO HELP YOU

GROW IN CONFIDENCE

1. In what area of your life do you feel stagnant? What can you do on purpose to move forward from that place?

2. Is there something you would really do, but you are afraid to move forward with it? What small step can you take to break stagnation and begin to overcome fear?

CONFIDENCE BOOSTER

Never be lacking in zeal, but keep your spiritual fervor, serving the Lord.

(Romans 12:11)

Whatever your hand finds to do, do it with all your might.

(Ecclesiastes 9:10)

So I commend the enjoyment of life, because there is nothing better for a person under the sun than to eat and drink and be glad. Then joy will accompany them in their toil all the days of the life God has given them under the sun.

(Ecclesiastes 8:15)

CHAPTER NINE

CONFIDENT PEOPLE REACH OUT TO OTHERS

Those who are happiest are those
who do the most for others.

People who live with confidence in God trust Him to meet their every need and to take care of everything that concerns them (Psalm 138:8). They are not overly focused on their own provision or well-being. They believe the promise of Philippians 4:L9 for themselves and want God to use them to help others experience it too. "And my God will meet all your needs according to the riches of his glory in Christ Jesus." Therefore they are happy to help or bless others when they see a chance to do so, in whatever way....big or small....may be needed. They know they can help people close to them in the simplest way by smiling and being friendly or by holding a door open when someone has their hands full. They also know that they can benefit people who live on the other side of the world by donating to missions or charities that work in underprivileged nations. They train themselves to look for needs of any kind, and they are quick to do whatever they can do to help.

People without confidence usually won't offer to help others because they fear being rejected. I recall wanting to pay for someone's grocery at Food 4 Less one night, and the person simply refused to let me do so. It was a bit embarrassing because other people saw what was going on, but I am not going to let an incident like that prevent me from reaching out to others. A less confident person might allow a situation such as that one make them fearful of trying again. It's our responsibility to do what we believe God is guiding us to do, no matter how other people respond.

Some individuals pass quietly through life, not making the impact they could make because they lack the confidence they need to make a difference in the world or in someone life, and to bless others. They spend their time and energy taking care of their needs and making sure they are provided for. They don't think much about doing something....even seemingly small....to make the world a better place. The fact is, though, that nothing they do is insignificant if it helps make some's life easier or their burden lighter.

While it is responsible to be wise stewards of our resources and to provide for ourselves and our families, the Bible also instructs us to help others and to be generous (Proverbs 22:9). Philippians 2:4 addresses this specifically, saying: "Let each of you look not only to his own interests, but also to the interests of others." We have opportunities every day to help people, if we will simply be aware of them and step up to do whatever we can do to assist.

Just think about it: Someone at your job, business or walking the streets that's hungry, need a place to sleep or even sick and need a helping hand. Someone in your life may be disappointed, and a smile or an encouraging word from you would lift their spirits. Someone you know may have lost a spouse recently, and they would love a phone call or a visit because they are lonely. Perhaps a neighbor had just been diagnosed with a debilitating disease, and a casserole, a bowl of fresh fruits, or a plate of muffins would be comforting. Or maybe a family at church is in danger of losing their home because one spouse lost their job and hasn't been able to find another one for months.

The bank is ready to foreclose on their loan, and they really have nowhere else to go. They are desperate and don't know what to do. Everyone tells them that God will provide, but no one is doing anything. Could you offer them a place to live or ask several other people to pitch in with you to meet this family's expenses for a month or two?

Many times, when we think of helping people, we think of obvious needs, such as the ones I have just mentioned. One place we sometimes forget to look when we think of people we can help is right under your own roof.

Perhaps your spouse or one of your children could use some affirmation or words of appreciation. Maybe a child is struggling in school and needs your undivided attention to help with their homework. You may not have to go very far to help or bless someone in a big way.

God is always eager to help and provide for people, but He works through other people....perhaps you. We are His hands, feet, arms, mouth, eyes, and ears. God does miracles, but He often does them through people with the confidence to say, "I would love to help you."

YOU CAN BE AN ADD-ER
OR A SUBTRACT-ER

When God created Adam and Eve, He blessed them and told them to be fruitful and multiply and use all the vast resources He gave to serve Himself and others (Genesis 1:28). So let me ask you. Are you being fruitful? When you get involved with people, do situations get better, not worse? Some people only take in life, and they never add anything. They don't even put a smile on someone else's face. I refuse to be that kind of person. I want to make people's lives better, and I'm sure you do too. It's a blessed way to live.

Jesus told the story of a man who had so much that all of his burns were full, with no room to hold any more. Instead of giving any of it away he decided to tear down the burns he had and just build bigger ones to collect more stuff for himself (Luke 12:16-18).

He could have chosen to use what he had to bless others, but he must have been a fearful, selfish man, who only had room in his life for himself (Luke 12:19). God called the man a fool and said, "This very night your life will be demanded from you. Then who will get what you have prepared for yourself?"(Luke 12:20). The man would die that night, and all he would leave behind were his wordy possession. He had an opportunity to make the world a better place. He could have added to many lives and put smiles on thousands of faces. Instead, he fearful and selfish cared only about himself.

Jesus said that if we want to be His disciples, we will lose sight of our personal interests and focus on serving Him (Mark 8:34). The minute we hear that we tend to think, what about me? If I forget myself, who will take care of me? Believe me when I say that God Himself will t6ake care of you. Everything you do for other people will come back to you and bring you joy, many times over. If you are willing to give yourself away, you will enjoy a much better life than you would ever experience if you stay overly focused on trying to take care of yourself.

I hope you will refuse to selfishly and fearfully pass through this life and do everything you can, in every way you can, for everyone that you can, as often as you can. If that is your goal, you will be one who makes the world a better place and put a smile on people faces.

Be courageous when you see someone in need, and start doing all you can to help others. Have confidence that God will meet all your needs, and begin to ask Him to give you the resources to meet the needs of people around you.

QUESTIONS TO HELP YOU

GROW IN CONFIDENCE

1. What can you expect to happen when you are generous, according to Luke 6:38?

2. Who can you bless this week? How?

CONFIDENCE BOOSTER

Give, and it will be given to you. A good measure, pressed down, shaken together and running over, will be poured into your lap. For with the measured to you.

(Luke 6:30)

If anyone has material possessions and sees a brother or sister in need but has no pity on them, how can the love of God be in that person?

(1 John 3:17)

CHAPTER TEN

LIVE YOUR LIFE WITH LOVE

Grace teaches us that God loves
because of who God is, no because
of who we are.

Have you ever wondered why some people are confident and others are not? Maybe they were raised in the same family and share many of the same experiences. Perhaps they read the same books and attend the same social events. Maybe they attend the same church and they hear the same Bible teaching each week. They may sing together in worship, or sit together in a prayer meeting. Even though they have similar experiences, some are strong and confident while others are not. There may be several reasons for this. Some people have received and embraced God's love for them the love He reveals to them directly and extends to them through other people while other still struggle to do so.

People who know they are loved are much more confident than those who don't. It helps to believed they have the love of God and the love of the important people in their lives, but even when they aren't surrounded by huge amounts of human love, God's love is enough. People who are convinced that God loves them possess and inner strength and a confidence that nothing else....can give, and nothing can take away. Consider Paul's words about the power of God,s love:

> For I am convinced that neither death nor life,
> Neither angels nor demons, neither the present
> Nor the future, nor any powers, neither height nor

Depth, nor anything else in all creation, will be able
To separate us from the love of God that is
in Christ Jesus. (Romans 8:39)

GOD LOVE FOR YOU

There is no limit to how confident you can become when you know first and foremost that God loves you unconditionally. When this truth is settled in your heart you will never again fear being rejected or unloved. You will rest in the fact that God loves and accepts you unconditionally, no matter what you do or how you may fail. God doesn't love it when we sin, but He never stop loving us. When you are not afraid of being unloved, you can live with remarkable boldness. Knowing you are loved will make whole, complete, and strong on the inside.

Everyone desires and need love and acceptance from God and from other people. Although not everyone will accept and love us, some will. We are wise to concentrate on those who don't. God certainly does love us, and He can provide others who love us too if we ask Him to lead us to people He wants in our lives and show us whom to bring into our circle of inclusion.

We can sense and know God's love as He reveals it to us in our hearts, but we also experience it through the people He gives us to walk with on our journey through life. I believe we need what I call divine connections, meaning relationships that God orchestrates and brings into our lives. These are people through whom He can show us His love, people who will pray for us and ask Him to help us, people who will encourage us with His Word.

I encourage you to pray about your circle of the friends. Don't just decide that you want to be part of a certain social group and then try to get into it. Instead, follow the leading of the Holy Spirit in choosing those with whom you want to associate closely with. He will help you recognize the people who will bless your life and whom you can bless in return, as you allow Him to guide you in relationships. God can give you favor with the people who are right for you, those who will add to your life and help develop godly character.

If you recognize the need for love in your life, the place to start is with God. He is a Father who wants to shower love and blessings upon His children. If your natural father did not love you properly, you can receive from God what you missed in your childhood. Love is the healing balm that the world needs, and God offers it freely and continuously. His love is unconditional. He does not love us if....He simply and for all times loves us. He loves us because He is kind and because He desires to show us His love.

A MESSAGE FROM THE AUTHOR

Dear Friends,

You are destined for greatness. God created you that way, and He has never changed His mind. In your hands you are holding a Book that can help you find your destiny. I believe my book can changed the destinies of everyone that read it from prison to throne rooms and from barrooms to banquet halls. The reason I said from prison because we all are in prison of the world if we don't have Jesus Christ our Lord and Savior in our lives.

The ink of the pages in my book can't do it. But God's words can, if you plant it in your heart, and confess your sins to Him. God's Word will separate you from the death of the world and place you in the flow of His life if you will "give attention to my words; Incline your ear to my sayings. Do not let them depart from your eyes; Keep them in the midst of your heart; For they are life to those who find them, And health to all their flesh" (Proverbs 4:20-22).

What makes my books different-it's words are filled with life, because they are God's Word. Other religious books are written to your head. But my books I write is written to your heart. Read the Bible as God talking straight to you as a Father. He loves you and wants the best for you. Don't be distracted by the arguments and theories men. People have worked hard at making the Bible complicated. It is quite simply a love letter from God to you. This is not bad mail. It's good news from cover to cover. God knows who you are and where you are. He knows why He created you. And He has a great plan to get you on the road to your destiny in Him. Just put your confidence in Him and He want let you down I can promise you that.

Remember God loves you. Jesus loves you...and I love you trust God.

John W. Manning

Printed in the United States
by Baker & Taylor Publisher Services